THE LIES WE TELL

THE LIES WE TELL

Mahendra Solanki

Shoestring Press

All rights reserved. No part of this work covered by the copyright herein may be reproduced or used in any means – graphic, electronic, or mechanical, including copying, recording, taping, or information storage and retrieval systems – without written permission of the publisher.

Printed by imprintdigital
Upton Pyne, Exeter
www.imprintdigital.net

Typeset by types of light
typesoflight@gmail.com

Published by Shoestring Press
19 Devonshire Avenue, Beeston, Nottingham, NG9 1BS
(0115) 925 1827
www.shoestringpress.co.uk

First published 2014
Copyright © Mahendra Solanki

The moral right of the author has been asserted

ISBN 978-1-910323-09-0

ACKNOWLEDGEMENTS

Acknowledgements are due to the editors of the following publications where some of the poems (in earlier versions) have appeared:

Critical Survey, *The Coffee House*, *The North*, *The Rialto*, *Temper* (University of Massachusetts), *The Rat's Mirror* with Matthew Caley et al (Ha'penny Press, Lapwing Publications), *Speaking English: Poems for John Lucas* (Five Leaves), *Miracle and Clockwork: the Best of Other Poetry Series Two* (Other Poetry), *Settling the Score* (East Midlands Arts), *Twelve Modern Young Indian Poets* (Lines Review), *The Yellow Nib: Modern English Poetry by Indians* (Queen's University, Belfast), *The Redbeck Anthology of British South Asian Poetry* (Redbeck Press), *The Harper Collins Book of English Poetry* (Harper Collins) and to the BBC where several of the poems were first broadcast.

'Fading from View: Hammershoi Interiors' appeared in a limited edition from Eyelet Books, an imprint of Shoestring Press in 2009.

The 'Riverside' poems were originally commissioned by The Riverside Arts Commission (TRAC) and Leicester

City Council's Permanent Art Collection. They were produced in collaboration with the artist Kay van Bellen. 'The Nottingham Mosaic' was commissioned by Nottingham City Council and Nottinham Castle Museum. 'Warnings' was commissioned by The King's Fund for the Waiting Room project and distributed as part of the Arts Council New Audiences Scheme.

I remain grateful to Tim Fulford, John Goodridge, Sarah Jackson, John Lucas, Sudeep Sen, Di Slaney, Pete Smith, Sam Ward and Gregory Woods for their continued encouragement and insightful comments during the writing of some of these poems.

I also offer this collection to the spirit of my former colleague, friend and poet, Michael Murphy (1965–2009) whose legacy remains, *awakening us from the loss of self that gathers in corners, aching to be of use.*

CONTENTS

i. forever marked

After a while you believe the lies you tell	3
Bol Bapu Bol	4
Bottle	5
Days	6
Eggs	7
Gaps	8
Black and White	9
Thirst	10
I wish I had asked	11

ii. for the grace of accuracy

Fading from View: Hammershoi Interiors

1 Old Woman at the Window	15
2 Bedroom (1890)	16
3 Interior, Frediksberg Alle (1900)	17
4 Two Figures (1898)	18
5 Interior (1893)	19
6 Interior, Strandgate 30	20

7 Interior, young woman seen from behind the drawing room	21
8 Interior, Strandgate 30	22
9 White Doors (1905)	23
10 Interior Courtyard (1905)	24
11 Interior, Bredgade 25 (1911)	25

Rothko	27
Body of Work	28
Untitled, 1950–52	29
Red on Maroon Mural Section 4, 1959	30

Anish Kapoor at The Royal Academy

When I am Pregnant	31
Non-Object (Door), 2008	32
Pillar	33
Mirror	34
Hive, 2009	35
Swayambh, 2007	36

Richard Long at the Tate

1 A Line Made by Walking	37
2 England, 1968	38
3 A Circle in Alaska, 1977	39

4	A Line in Scotland	40
5	Site – Specific	41
6	Transference	42
7	Karoo Line, 2004	43
8	Alpine Stones, 2000/Snowdonia Stones, 2006	44
9	Waterlines, 2003	45

iii. Commissions, Instructions, Warnings

Warnings	49
Letting Go	50
Steps	51
Both reminders, a jolt	52
County Clare	53
Card Players	54
Pots	55
Nottingham Mosaic	56
Tongue	57
A stranger, well received	58
Chutney	59
Fruit	60
Elephants	61
Wishes	62
from The Riverside Commission	63
Last Self-Portrait	65

for Hannah and Ansuya

We had a kingdom
Or did I dream it?

We keep coming back and coming back
To the real …

                          Wallace Stevens

i
forever marked

About ten years ago one thought one had got rid of that, one thought one had entered a new world; one was making one's own life.

V.S. Naipaul

After a while you believe the lies you tell

That bump on your head –
did your father really throw you down the stairs?

– that story about your name and how,
not able to read, write or speak English
you copied the Sikh girl's name as your own –
and you say no one noticed
until you moved to another school.

And that one about how
you said you'd care for me
and would die
rather than do any harm?

There are no pictures of you as a child,
no way of checking if that lump was there before.
There are no old exercise books with the girl's name.
There is no piece of paper with your promise –

just this ring, this bruise and the words I recall.

Bol Bapu Bol

I wait for you to speak
bol bapu bol
speak father speak

you appear in a dream
but not to speak

you are with my wife
in an open-topped truck

I am running behind
shouting   I throw a rolled-
up bed up to my wife

The driver (an old teacher) doesn't stop

she is at home when I arrive
I shout   I pull her by the throat
I push her hard against the wall

you came not to speak

but to admire
to nod   at your handiwork

Bottle

You tell that story again
of how you came in
and saw him grabbing
her by her hair

you say that she is bleeding
from her mouth
her sari coming undone
no Hanuman to save her

and you stare, fixed again
and you're holding
an ice-cold bottle
of milk, unable to move
and you say he laughs
saying, 'You daren't.
You're *just* like a girl.'

Days

Your days are counted out
in a row for me
a pull of dates
torn from a calendar:
an abacus of hope

Eggs

I make it the way you did:
cracked eggs spiced with
nuggets of red chilli,
catching my breath.

Each plate, stained
like my fingers with
turmeric, forever marked.

Gaps

I walk into your room
after they took you away
looking for anything that's
still a part of you, imagining
a clip of nail, a wisp
of hair to be yours – trapped
in the gaps in the floor;
nothing to grasp,
nothing to hold on.

Black and White

Can it ever be put right
remembering how you hit him
over the head with a brass pot
as he climbed on top of you?
And did he bleed? And did he leave?
It's hard to recall such de-
tail, in black and white.

Thirst

And what good will come
to tell now, of how for years
your mother took you to see
the priest, who once alone
with you, talked you out of
your shorts, and with you emptied,
would plead for you to piss into
his mouth; his thirst not quenched?

I wish I had asked

We argue each time we meet
we cannot agree on anything.

*Yes, I read your book, not meaning to;
someone had left it behind.*

I wish I had asked of what you thought
about how I described ourselves.

ii

for the grace of accuracy

The painter's vision is not a lens,
It trembles to caress the light

                Robert Lowell

Fading from View: Hammershoi Interiors

1   Old Woman at the Window (1885)

I see you again after years,
still at the window
your back to me; waiting.

The room behind you floats,
it's almost as if you're leaving,
fading before my eyes,
the light from the window
pulling you away.

2 Bedroom (1890)

You look out of the windows
much younger, again
waiting between
two beds and
a floating floor
rising above,
framed by curtains.
The glass mirror remains blank.

3 Interior, Frediksberg Alle (1900)

This room is our room,
dark, despite the light
straining from the windows.
Never enough light.

Covered chairs, old furniture,
you standing in the corner;
both waiting for the other to speak.

4 Two Figures (1898)

The only thing to shine in this darkness
is the ring of gold on her right hand finger,
against the washed grey of the tablecloth.

She looks (not at him)
but neither is she turning away.
Both have given up talking in the dark.

5   Interior (1893)

She's reading a book;
a diary, as always
her back to me;
her hair tied up,
the white door ajar.

6   Interior, Strandgade 30

Always the same view
and a woman's back.
Another little interior.

The light, casting
the wrong shadows,
cropping the furniture.

7 Interior, young woman seen from behind in the drawing room

She stands, facing a wall,
holding a dinner plate.
A bowl rests on the piano.

Her hair is plaited and pinned up;
the back of her dress not fully fastened.

8 Interior, Strandgade 30

We live in different rooms.
I see you through your open door
facing into the light coming
from the far window.

I live in my room
with one chair and
two photographs of
our two girls, fading from view.

Our marriage is now a coupling
of stories to tell our daughters
to point at figures in a painting.

9 White doors (1905)

Three white doors, open wide
in empty rooms;
each a way out,
each a reason for not staying.

10 Interior Courtyard (1905)

You at last come into view
at the open window,
head bowed, fist clenched;
a face resigned.

11 Interior, Belgrade 25 (1911)

The table, a stumbling block –
always between us –

what do I say to you
you so far away?

Rothko

When they found his body in the morning
He was lying face up on the floor
In a six by eight stretch of blood;
Arms outstretched, ready for hanging.

Body of Work

These parts of me,
the head, the heart
are of no use now

the rush of blood
stopped in its tracks
the mouth stunned
after so much talk
swallow these marks
these slabs of paint:
stare at what remains.

Untitled, 1950–52

This is the body in bloom,
between a green flower-
ing, and a lilac burial.

Red on Maroon Mural Section 4, 1959

No one else could ever be admitted here, since this gate was made only for you.
Franz Kafka

This is your door, a way out.
It glows at your approach,
its silver mouth opening
wide, for your release.

Anish Kapoor at The Royal Academy

A word can't substitute for an image, but is equal to it

John Baldessari

When I am Pregnant, 1992

This is how the world
comes into being:
when you weren't looking

Non-Object (Door), 2008

You come and go
forever changing;
each woman
turning into you.

Pillar

I look back
(against all advice)
as you change;
pulling me
(against my will).

Mirror

This is the child
I sent away,
staring at me
from a distance.

I return his gaze;
how can I call him mine?

Mirror (overheard)

'When you are down
you do not see yourself'

Hive

Knowing what you know
would you choose
to go down the hole
(to be born again)?

Swayambh

We all ask,
'when does it come through?'
We all wait,
not satisfied.

It is a train, sure as wax,
coming for you.

Richard Long at the Tate

1 A Line Made by Walking

This is a line, made
by others before
you, to guide you
through your uncertainty

2 England, 1968

Two lines in an open field
to mark as home –
if only it was that simple

3 A Circle in Alaska

This is a laying out
in the round –
a circling of driftwood
on the shore
as the tide comes in –
no guard against anything

4 A Line in Scotland, 1981

Nobody's looking –
relax – let go:
these stones are
upright witnesses

5 Site – Specific

Wherever you look
whatever you see,
it is the same:
a coming together of lines,
of boundaries and turns,
all going round in circles

6 Transference

After a while you find what
you're looking for,
over and over

7 Karoo Line, 2004

I come to these open places
between walking and rest
no longer sure
whether it is to find you
or to lose myself

8 Alpine Stones 2000/Snowdonia Stones 2006

If these stones
are guides
for the lost,
god help us

9 Waterlines

This is my last wish:
you and me
coming together
returning to the sea

iii

Commissions, Instructions and Warnings

> Back and forth, back and forth
> Goes the tock, tock, tock
>
> Robert Lowell

Warnings

How many times have I told you?
Look where you're going. Walk don't run.
I repeat to myself warnings
that are out of place and too late.

I have never got used to this:
the rush here, all else forgotten;
always fearing the worst, knowing
this pain will pass. For you to smile.

Letting Go: for Hannah

I rejoice in your abandonment.
Gripped tight in my arms,
you roll with me over the edge;
unlearning habits of restraint.

Steps: for Ansuya

Tread carefully
    Let my cheers guide your steps
Should you still stumble
    Let my arms break your fall

Both reminders, a jolt

"He had a tremendous talent for happiness."
"She has a sense of fun and full of life."

The first, a widow talking about her husband,
the other, someone talking about our daughter.

One, a reason to celebrate the dead.
The second, an instruction to the living.

County Clare

That which I could not find
I discover in this land:
a love as wild as the sea
and as constant as the rain.

Card Players

Two men sit in chairs
face to face, but do not
look at each other.

Rather, they stare at cards,
as still as a glass of water,
as quiet as a bowl of fruit.

Time to call the other man's
bluff, each knowing all the time
a wrong move means losing all.

Pots

"I don't think I know you"

I know you by taste,
as rich as the earth
from which you were born.

I know you by touch,
by your folding curves
and your arching back,

by your still warm smell
burnt into your scarred skin.

Nottingham Mosaic

        the   mind's

    in   eye

trace   a

                                  braille

                        of

              what

        once

   was

here

seek   dead

    the   the

          living among

Tongue

I utter your words –
words as alien
as your tongue
in my mouth –
making them mine

A Stranger, well received

You could not call him one of your own,
his face all mottled pink and red;
even in summer, in tweeds and brogues.

But here, I almost embrace him
as he translates a menu
as foreign as the food:
stewed testicles, stomach of geese,
liver force-fed on maize.

Chutney

High priest, harvester
of fruit, anointer of
oils, master of spice
you mix and store
you wait and pray

you can only tell
what is sweet or
sour by swallowing
it whole; where does
sweetness lie, when
does the sourness end?

Fruit

"Do I have to feel something?"

To you it's round and smooth.
Touch is literal; one handed.
There is no room to feel
the object's curve, the
gash that trails to a tip.

I offer you my hands
but hold back in fear
you might push them away.

Here, I offer myself to you:
unpeel me the way you
would an over-ripe fruit;
bite, let the juices run.

Elephants

If elephants do not forget,
it is because they have
very little to remember.

We remember even less
of words said or heard,
jumbled or partially recalled.

I suppose we remember best
the odd detail: a man
squatting in an open field,
the ugly crease in a smile,
the girl staring out of a train;
the one remaining tree.

Wishes

What do you think about
When you think about me?

I think about your wishes

About my tongue inside you
About the wind outside
About your scent around me

About the give of figs opened
About the feel of warm asparagus
About your mouth as my container

About how wishes come in threes

from **The Riverside Commission**

i.

the A frame stretched tight
against a familiar sky

take a step, a start

ii.

a canal, a river
through a lost green corridor
a well-kept secret

iii.

a man runs on this path
between grass and water
like a feverish race horse
blinkered against distractions

iv.

a to and fro
a giant see-saw rocking

a give and take:
the hiss and spill of the past

v.

we who left behind our lands
we who crossed the black ocean
we who miss the open fields and running water

we seek comfort in this pull of green
we seek rest in this flowing bed

Last Self-Portrait

That is me one of these days
without the hat, the shorn beard,
the hollowed cheeks, staring
blindly into the lens, into your gaze;
standing between the stopped
clock and the well-made bed.

Mahendra Solanki was born in Nairobi of Indian parents and his work draws upon this background to locate his poetry. He has worked in publishing, bookselling, adult and community education and the theatre. Until recently, he taught English and Creative Writing at Nottingham Trent University as well as directing a long-established MA in Writing. Since the publication of his first collection, *Shadows of My Making* in 1986, his poems have appeared widely in magazines and anthologies in Britain and abroad and have been broadcast by the BBC. His other publications include *What You Leave Behind* (1996). He is presently a Royal Literary Fund Fellow at the University of Warwick.